Literary Circles of Washington

Also in this series:

LITERARY
CIRCLES
OF
WASHINGTON

Edith Nalle Schafer

STARRHILL PRESS
Washington, D.C.

Starrhill Press, Inc., publisher
P.O. Box 21365
Washington, D.C. 20009
(202) 387-9805

Illustrations by Jonel Sofian.
Maps by Deb Norman.
Hand-marbled paper by Iris Nevins, Sussex, N.J.

The author wishes to note that this book concerns itself with
Washington's literary past and mentions living writers only in passing.

Library of Congress Cataloging-in-Publication Data

Schafer, Edith Nalle.
   Literary circles of Washington / Edith Nalle Schafer. — 1st ed.
     p.   cm.
   Includes index.
   ISBN 0-913515-92-2
   1. American literature—Washington (D.C.)—History and criticism.
2. Literary landmarks—Washington (D.C.)—Guidebooks. 3. Authors,
American—Washington (D.C.)—Biography. 4. Walking—Washington
(D.C.)—Guidebooks. 5. Washington (D.C.)—Intellectual life.
6. Washington (D.C.) in literature. I. Title.
PS253.D6S33   1993
810.9'9753—dc20   93-34514
                                    CIP

Printed in the United States of America
First edition
9 8 7 6 5 4 3 2 1

For Jack
il miglior fabbro

Contents

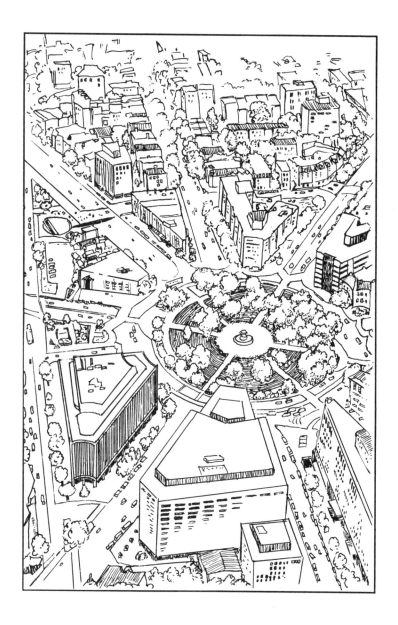

Introduction

WHAT WITH flux in summer and ague in winter, fetid malarial swamps, unpaved and unlit streets and pig wallows on the Mall, it must have seemed a poor excuse for a capital city. "As in 1800 and 1850, so in 1860," wrote Henry Adams, "the same rude colony was camped in the same forest, with the same unfinished Greek temples for workrooms, and sloughs for roads." Washington had no cultural or commercial reason to exist; it was just a place for government. Grandiose, incomplete, it was an idea imposed on a wilderness.

But from the beginning Pierre Charles L'Enfant's grand design envisioned a city of majestic avenues radiating out from stately circles. A noble city would rise up, and in the cozy neighborhoods formed by the intersections of the avenues, people would live.

It is a city of neighborhoods, washed over again and again by the influx of clever and interesting men and women who give life in Washington its peculiarly satisfying quality. As they arrive, so they depart, giving an impression of nimbleness to a city of monuments. Even ordinary citizens not involved in the complex government layering derive vicarious excitement from the proximity to power. Washingtonians like brushing against great events, and they are not all faceless gray bureaucrats, in spite of what you've been told. There is a literary life here, and there has been from the very beginning.

Think of it as the alabaster city beside a shining river, the city on a hill, the place Dickens called the city of magnificent intentions—implying, of course, that it didn't quite succeed. Think of it as the last best hope, grant it grandeur and, as you walk the streets of its literary past, find it winsome.

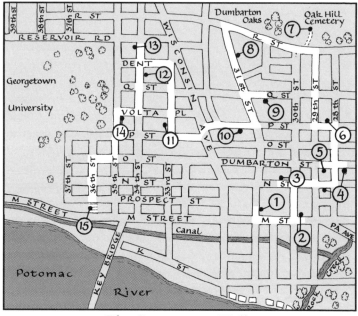

The Georgetown Walk

1. Booked Up: 1209 31st Street, NW
2. Louisa May Alcott: northeast corner of 30th and M Streets
3. Jacqueline Kennedy: 3017 N Street
4. Joseph Alsop: 2806 N and 2770 Dumbarton Avenue
5. Drew Pearson: 2820 Dumbarton Avenue
6. Dean Acheson: 2805 P Street
7. John Howard Payne: Oak Hill Cemetery
8. Katherine Garrison Chapin: 1669 31st Street
9. Sinclair Lewis: 3028 Q Street
10. Katherine Anne Porter: 3106 P Street
11. Archibald MacLeish: 1520 33rd Street
12. St.-John Perse: 1621 34th Street
13. Tohoga House, 1686 34th Street
14. Walter Lippmann: 1527 35th Street
15. The Exorcist Steps

Fabled Georgetown

FULL OF AMBIGUITIES, inherently congenial and interesting, Georgetown has a hidden life, goes its own way, and has nothing at all to do with the tawdry commerce of its main streets. The impassive exteriors of the handsome federal houses and small row houses scarcely hint at the well-appointed and interesting life within. Residents here want to be anonymous, not to each other but to the tour buses. Over time somebody famous has lived in every other house.

There is a street life. On weekends the freak-show, carnival atmosphere of Wisconsin Avenue contrasts oddly with the good gray residents going about their ordinary business on the side streets.

In his wonderful book, *Spring in Washington*, Louis Halle says that Georgetown was where the West began. The gateway to a limitless continent, it was where the men of the eighteenth century changed into deerskin. A tobacco port with square-riggers in the harbor at the turn of the century, by the end of the nineteenth century it had changed from a country village into a congenial, convenient residential area for the growing city next door. In the 1930s and 1940s the gathering troops of the New Deal and then World War II contributed to the long renaissance that pretty much continues to this day. Georgetown considers itself noteworthy, special. And so it is.

To begin your exposure to Georgetown gently and in a fitting manner, start at Booked Up (owners: Marcia Carter and Larry McMurtry, author of, for example, *Lonesome Dove*) at 1209 31st Street. Booked Up offers old and rare books and modern first editions. Here, as in a scholar's dream, is a mellow room with bookcases to the ceiling where the gleam of the late sun on leather bindings complements the patina of old furniture and Italian altar candles. The aura pays homage to the life of the mind.

Leaving Booked Up, proceed down the hill and left along M Street to the northeast corner of M and 30th. Here we disconnect from the present and enter history.

In 1862 when the country was deep in civil war, Dorothea Dix, the country's first supervisor of nurses, issued a circular calling for women between the ages of thirty-five and fifty, strong, matronly, sober, neat and industrious. If they could produce two testimonials to their excellent morals, they would receive transportation and forty cents a day. LOUISA MAY ALCOTT (1832–1888) was young, but she made up for it in matronliness and sobriety.

At home in Concord, Massachusetts, Alcott felt keenly the need to fill the economic void left by her impractical father, who worked largely at being an itinerant transcendentalist sage. Besides, she had, as she said, a romantic taste for heroism and "ghastliness." She found them.

She came to Washington and was immediately assigned to the Union Hotel Hospital, a converted tavern on the northeast corner of 30th and M Streets. It was an awful place. A seedy building contained rows of sagging beds, dirty floors and broken, unwashed windows. Some fifty miles away, the battle of Fredericksburg was raging in the rain. Within days wagons of wounded men began to arrive. Lying on pallets, they lined the halls.

Alcott had brought games to entertain the soldiers and copies of Dickens's novels, which she pictured herself reading aloud to convalescing men in sunny hospital rooms. The reality was something else. In fact, she did recite passages of *David Copperfield*, from memory, to a soldier having his arms removed without ether.

The work was grueling, and there was no respite. Inevitably she became a patient herself, contracting typhoid and pneumonia. The medical wisdom of the time called for massive doses of laxatives. Louisa was given calomel, a mercury compound that caused loss of teeth and hair; her tongue swelled to four or five times its normal size and protruded from her mouth. Eventually the emetic caused trembling, weakness, anxiety, delirium, and general deterioration. The doctors swore by it.

Alcott's father came and took her home delirious. Tragically, she never really got her health back. She had been in Washington four weeks.

Out of her experience came *Hospital Sketches* (1863), a collection of her letters home. It was her first successful book and was followed in a few years by *Little Women*, whose enormous popularity did indeed enable Louisa to give her family security and comfort.

To come back into the twentieth century, walk up 30th to N and go left briefly to 3017 N, where Jacqueline Kennedy, widow of the author of *Profiles in Courage*, lived after the president's death. At 2806 N and also at 2720 Dumbarton lived columnist **JOSEPH ALSOP** (1910–1989), a champion entertainer and mixer of lively guests. His basic rule: no more than one bore per dozen guests. With his brother Stewart, he wrote the syndicated column, "Matter of Fact." It was to Alsop's Dumbarton Avenue house that John Kennedy came looking for a party the night of his inauguration.

Columnist **DREW PEARSON** (1897–1969), master of the art of sustained hostility, knew everyone, spared no one, and had a world-class network of sources, whom he never offended and never revealed. He was a muckraker-crusader who took on any public figure he wanted to and filled his columns (eight syndicated ones a week) with vigorous abuse.

Pearson kept the level of vituperation and obloquy high in his books, *Washington Merry-Go-Round* and *More Merry-Go-Round*, which were accordingly very successful. The post office delivered a letter addressed simply to "The S.O.B." to 2820 Dumbarton Avenue. There in his beautiful garden Pearson served very dry martinis known as Titanics because they were so large and went down so easily. At his Merry-Go-Round Farm on the Potomac River he sold manure in bags marked "Pearson's Best Manure—Better than the Column—All Cow and No Bull."

On the corner of 28th and O is the charming and beloved Francis Scott Key Bookshop, a neighborhood store.

Continuing up 28th to the corner of P Street, look left to 2805 P, the handsome house that belonged for many years to **DEAN ACHESON** (1893–1971) and his wife, the artist Alice Acheson. Acheson was President Truman's secretary of state, a lawyer and the author of several books, including Pulitzer Prize winner *Present at the Creation* (1969).

The entrance to Oak Hill Cemetery is at the top of 30th Street. This steep and wooded site above Rock Creek Park has a lovely little Renwick chapel and is the final resting place of, among many others, John Howard Payne.

Who now remembers the strange, sad story of **JOHN HOWARD PAYNE** (1791–1852), a once popular writer? Payne was a child prodigy and the foremost actor-playwright of the early American theater. Perpetually impoverished, he wrote more than sixty plays, many of them performed abroad, where he was sometimes a success, sometimes in debtor's prison.

He wrote and translated what he called Melo-Dramas: *Adeline; or The Victim of Seduction, Julia; or The Wanderer* (which he wrote and saw produced at age fifteen) and *Clari; or The Maid of Milan.* This last play included the song, "Home, Sweet Home."

In 1832, after almost twenty years in Europe, Payne returned to this country. Ten years later, with the help of Daniel Webster, he got appointed consul to Tunis, where he ultimately died.

You might think the saga of John Howard Payne would end there, but it doesn't. Thirty-one years later, William W. Corcoran, who as a boy had admired Payne's acting, had his body dug up and brought back to Washington in a lead coffin. Wanting to honor the author of "Home, Sweet Home," Corcoran had the coffin drawn by four white horses to the Corcoran Gallery of Art (then located in the Renwick Gallery, 17th and Pennsylvania Avenue), where it lay in state. Then he organized a funeral procession led by President Chester A. Arthur and including the cabinet, the Supreme Court, important senators and congressmen and other dignitaries to Oak Hill Cemetery. John Philip Sousa led the Marine Corps Band in "Home, Sweet Home." All sang.

A pedestal with the bust of Payne commissioned by Corcoran stands to the right just inside the gates at 30th and R Streets. Corcoran is buried on the other side of the cemetery.

Next to the cemetery, moving west along R, is a fine grassy sward, Montrose Park, and beyond it the incomparable Dumbarton Oaks with its beautiful little museum of Byzantine and pre-Columbian art and its world-class gardens. Open every day at 2 p.m. and not to be missed. The gardens were laid out by the great garden designer Beatrix Farrand, who was the niece of novelist Edith Wharton.

Now proceed down 31st Street passing 1669, where the poet Katherine Garrison Chapin (wife of Attorney General Francis Biddle) lived and entertained her fellow poets. She provided a genuine literary salon that has not been duplicated since she left Washington in 1973.

Pass Tudor Place on your right. Tudor Place was lived in by the family of George Washington's wife, Martha Custis Washington, from 1816 until 1984, when it became a private museum operated by the Tudor Place Foundation. A National Historic Landmark, it is open to the public by appointment. It, too, is an oasis in the city.

SINCLAIR LEWIS (1885–1951) was never sure whether the American small town was the worst or the best of places.

In 1919 he was a long way from Sauk Centre, Minnesota, his hometown, looking for a place where he and his wife could afford to live while he finished *Main Street*. He found it at 1814 16th Street. Lewis felt Washington to be the perfect place for writing, "with neither the country and lake tempting one out to play, as in Minnesota, nor the noise and phone calls of New York." He joined the Cosmos Club, a meeting place for local intellectuals (then located in the Dolley Madison House on Lafayette Square), and developed a tendency to invite virtual strangers home with him.

Poet Elinor Wylie was among his new friends, as were the Dean Achesons. One evening when the latter were entertaining in their house at 1830 Corcoran Street, an apparition in the guise of an Armenian rug merchant burst in and tried to sell their astonished guests some motheaten rugs. It was just Sinclair Lewis taking a break from writing *Main Street*.

Main Street was about the stifling, complacent atmosphere, what Lewis felt to be "the ghetto-like confinement," of the small town.

3028 Q Street: Sinclair Lewis

When its heroine, Carol Kennicutt, finally rebelled and made her escape, she fled to—where else?—Washington. For her as for Lewis it seemed a magical place.

When Lewis delivered *Main Street* to his publisher, Alfred Harcourt, he hoped it would sell ten thousand copies. In fact, it was a sensation, reaching two million readers by 1922. If that many people liked it, was it a work of art? Lewis wondered.

Success had its compensations, and 1926 found the Lewises in a handsome Georgetown house at 3028 Q Street. His marriage was breaking up, and Lewis was writing *Elmer Gantry*. Between 1920 and 1929 Lewis wrote *Main Street*, *Babbitt*, *Arrowsmith*, *Elmer Gantry* and *Dodsworth*.

In 1930 he won the Nobel Prize for Literature, the first American to do so. By then he had left Washington. His marriage to journalist Dorothy Thompson and a lot of drinks were still ahead, but his best work had been done.

Here's a tidbit to ponder at 3106 P Street. There Elinor Wylie rang the doorbell of her friend Katherine Anne Porter, saying she intended to kill herself and Porter was the only one she wanted to say goodbye to. Porter responded, "Well, goodbye, Elinor," and closed the door.

KATHERINE ANNE PORTER (1890–1980) then added Elinor Wylie's name to a list of people who had tried to enlist her sympathy by threatening suicide.

The story is probably apocryphal. Anyway, Katherine Anne Porter was not such a stranger to life's cuffs and blows that she could afford an Olympian attitude. Porter spent most of her life trying to free herself from the effects of a loveless childhood, resentment of her poor and undistinguished origins, and a susceptibility to expecting solutions from relationships with men. To this end, as a young woman, she invented a past, giving herself a new name and an aristocratic family background.

Flowering Judas, the collection of short stories published in 1930, established Porter as a writer. In 1937 came *Noon Wine*, and in 1939 *Pale Horse, Pale Rider*. She was a natural storyteller with a sure sense of language. Her discipline and talent stayed with her through endless wanderings and disastrous marriages and love affairs, between the kisses and the wine.

High strung, beautiful ("she looked like a peacock who had fluttered down in a barnyard," a graduate student recalled), Porter knew everyone and was always involved in the cultural life of wherever she happened to be. In revolutionary Mexico in the 1920s she coped with the drunken, self-destructive behavior of Hart Crane, and in Germany in the 1930s she argued about race with Hermann Goering. Robert Penn Warren, Allen Tate and Caroline Gordon, Glenway Westcott, Eudora Welty, Edith Sitwell, J. F. Powers, Wallace Stegner, Archibald MacLeish and his wife and the French poet St.-John Perse were her friends. She and Elinor Wylie drank gin out of teacups in speakeasies together when they were between lovers.

She was pleased when Archibald MacLeish appointed her Fellow of Regional American Literature at the Library of Congress to fill poet and novelist John Peale Bishop's unfinished term. In January 1944, when she arrived in Washington to begin work, she called the Tates to come pick her up at Union Station. When they demurred saying they were too drunk, she took a cab to the house in Anacostia they shared with novelist Brainard Cheney and his wife. The house was known as "The Birdcage" because it was like a nest of singing birds.

The singing birds were soon at each other's throats. Porter couldn't take it, nor could they take her. The Tates found her a place as a boarder with young artist Marcella Comès Winslow and her family at 3106 P Street in Georgetown. Winslow painted writers and they came through her house in profusion. In the 1940s and '50s the P Street house was an informal literary salon distinguished by Robert Penn Warren, Mark Van Doren and the poets from the Library of Congress.

Room was always found for Eudora Welty when she came to town. Living with the Winslows turned out to be a happy arrangement.

Porter soon met Charles Shannon, a soldier just back from the South Pacific and stationed at nearby Fort Belvoir, a man much younger than she, with whom she had an idyllic love affair. Of Shannon—of lovers in general—she wrote: they are "transfigured with a light of such blinding brilliance all natural attributes disappear and are replaced by those usually associated with archangels at least. They are beautiful, flawless in temperament, witty, intelligent, charming, of such infinite grace, sympathy and courage, I always wondered how they could have come from such absurdly inappropriate families." And, "It is no good going into details for while it lasts there simply aren't any." He gave her armfuls of white roses.

He went back to his wife. Of the endings of love affairs she wrote, "Hell-fire is just under the crust of the flowery meadow."

In 1962 came the huge success of Porter's only novel, the long-aborning *Ship of Fools*. It brought her all the prizes that had eluded her and, together with the movie made from it, abundant money. She bought her dream house with stately rooms, lush lawns and a rose garden at 3601 49th Street in Spring Valley. It was a nice denouement to a hardscrabble life, but she saw herself with detachment. "I wouldn't have missed the life I've had, just as it was, for anything. . . . I read lately an observation by Anthony Trollope: 'Success is a necessary misfortune of life, but it is only to the very unfortunate that it comes early.'"

In 1975, in her mid-eighties, she moved into an apartment at 6100 Westchester Park Drive in College Park, Maryland, and in the last year of her life, to the Carriage Hill Nursing Home in Silver Spring, where she died in 1980. Her papers and books are housed in the Katherine Anne Porter Room of the University of Maryland.

If handsome, bright, competitive, athletic, well-to-do, gifted **ARCHIBALD MACLEISH** (1892–1982) had an affliction, it was an embarrassment of aptitudes. A man of passionate social conviction, he wanted to serve his country and he wanted to write great poetry. When he mixed his lyric gift with his causes, his poetry was the loser. "Griefs, not grievances," said Robert Frost, "are the stuff of poetry."

As a young man Archie got all the glittering prizes. On the day he was offered a partnership in the law firm of his choice, he tendered his resignation and took his young wife and two small children to Paris to see if he could write poetry. After five years in France (boxing with Hemingway, vacationing in Antibes), he was a major poet.

There ensued three Pulitzer Prizes, numerous medals and honors, stints as star writer for *Fortune*, librarian of congress, assistant secretary of state under Franklin D. Roosevelt, distinguished teacher of writing at Harvard. And all the time he was a decent, kind and balanced man.

It was MacLeish who, with consummate diplomacy, got Ezra Pound out of St. Elizabeth's Hospital. And he did it although, as he wrote Hemingway, "I have never had anything from Pound but vituperation and obscenity."

In Georgetown the MacLeishes lived at 1520 33rd Street, not far from his dear friend Dean Acheson and his old mentor from Harvard Law School, Supreme Court Justice Felix Frankfurter.

When he was Librarian of Congress MacLeish offered asylum to the poet, **ST.-JOHN PERSE** (1887–1975). Perse was the pen name of Alexis Léger, a Frenchman with two distinct lives, poet and diplomat, both distinguished. In 1940, opposed to appeasement, Léger fled the Nazis and gratefully accepted the job MacLeish created for him cataloging the French holdings of the Library of Congress.

Léger grew up on a family-owned island off Guadeloupe; his Hindu nurse was, in secret, a priestess of Shiva. Educated in France, Léger became a diplomat and was posted to China, where he rented a temple in the hills as a refuge. He traveled widely—South Sea islands, Central Asia—and became French foreign minister Aristide

Briand's right-hand man with the title of Secretary-General of the Ministry of Foreign Affairs and Ambassador of France (1932–1940). He lost his French citizenship in 1940 because of his stand against the appeasement of Germany.

That was Alexis Léger. St.-John Perse was a major poet. Like his life, his writing was exotic, influenced by his interest in early pagan mythology. His themes were solitude and exile. *Anabase* (1924) was translated by T. S. Eliot in 1930. *Exil* was simply handed to MacLeish one day to repay his kindness. MacLeish sent it to *Poetry*, where it was published in French in 1942. A 1949 translation by Denis Devlin confirmed Perse's reputation for readers of English. The poems are incantatory, hymnlike, addressed not to God but to the scope of man's triumphal experience. Perse won the Nobel Prize for Literature in 1960.

Léger's French citizenship was restored in 1945, but he didn't return to France until 1959, and after that he divided his time between France and America. When here, he lived at 1621 34th Street.

Just up 34th Street on the northwest corner of Reservoir Road is Tohoga House, where lived the fictional Pollit family in Christina Stead's fine 1940 novel *The Man Who Loved Children*.

The great jurist Oliver Wendell Holmes remarked to a clever and ambitious young journalist, "You young men seem to think that if you sit on the world long enough you will hatch something out. But you're wrong." But **WALTER LIPPMANN** (1889–1974) didn't believe him, or in any case didn't stop trying to make sense of events and over a long and productive career never stopped trying to hatch something out.

James Reston, long the Washington bureau chief of the *New York Times*, said of him that he "nourished the national dialogue on great subjects for over half a century." Relentlessly social as well as extremely able, Lippmann talked, listened, wrote, provoked, and opined at an endless series of big cocktail parties and small dinners.

When Lippmann moved from New York to Washington in 1917 with a new wife and a new job, he took up residence in a red brick house at 1727 19th Street. That establishment was a bachelor house, a kind of commune for bright young men in government. It didn't occur to Lippmann that it was an inappropriate place to take a bride. He liked his social life to have certain basic ingredients: clever conversation and gossip, attractive women and intelligent men. The half dozen bachelors gave continual parties for everyone who was famous, important or interesting. Justice Holmes, a frequent visitor, named it the "House of Truth."

In 1931 Lippmann left Washington to launch his extremely successful, widely syndicated column, "Today and Tomorrow," for the *New York Herald Tribune*. He had become the real thing—a pundit.

In 1937, after twenty years of a comfortable, lifeless marriage, Lippmann fell in love with his best friend's wife, Helen Armstrong. They married in 1938 and to get away from the gossip and acrimony in New York, moved to Washington and rented the Alexander Graham Bell house at 1527 35th Street on the corner of Volta Place. They were to live there for seven years until Helen Lippmann found her dream house. By this time Lippmann had published *A Preface to Politics* (1913), *Public Opinion* (1922), *A Preface to Morals* (1929) and *The Good Society* (1937). More books and two Pulitzer Prizes were still to come.

One of the Lippmanns' contributions to the Washington social scene was an annual New Year's Eve party at their elegant Tudor house at 3525 Woodley Road, where they moved in 1945. The luminous guests included Senator William Fulbright, *Washington Post* publisher Philip Graham and his wife Katherine Graham, French Ambassador Henri Bonnet, National Gallery curator John Walker and art collector Duncan Phillips. Later Philip Graham observed that at midnight when the guests joined hands, sang "Auld Lang Syne" and kissed each other, he always seemed to be holding hands with a small bowlegged diplomat.

To the west, with its dreaming spires and Gothic arches towering above the river, lies Georgetown University. A significant presence in the community, not the least of its claims to fame is the original handwritten manuscript of Mark Twain's *Tom Sawyer* tucked safely away in a vault in the library.

At the southwest corner of Prospect and 36th Streets used to stand Prospect Cottage, a charming Carpenters Gothic house lived in by **EMMA DOROTHY ELIZA NEVITTE SOUTHWORTH** (1819–1899).

The heroes and heroines of the novels of E. D. E. N. Southworth are not household words anymore and neither is she. Before the 1930s Mrs. Southworth was an enormously popular writer. She wrote seventy-three novels with stock characters and predictable endings, many of which sold more than a million copies. Southworth was aware that her sentimental and melodramatic plots were praised immoderately, and she claimed she would have written differently if freed from financial pressure.

Frederick Southworth took his bride to a cabin on the Wisconsin frontier and left her there for long periods of time with their two small children and howling wolves. Eventually he left her for good.

She returned home to Washington, taught school and supplemented her income by writing. *Retribution* was one of the first novels to be serialized in the *National Era*, making literary history in 1849 and spurring Southworth on.

Success enabled her to buy Prospect Cottage, which became a rendezvous for local literati. During the Civil War it was turned into a hospital, and President Lincoln sometimes slept there on his way to and from the battlefields. When Harriet Beecher Stowe negotiated with the *National Era* for publication of *Uncle Tom's Cabin*, Southworth put her up at Prospect Cottage. They became fast friends.

E. D. E. N. Southworth is buried in Oak Hill Cemetery, not far from John Howard Payne.

Right next to the former site of Prospect Cottage are the infamous Exorcist Steps, which have passed into the language from the eponymous thriller (1971) and movie by William Peter Blatty. The steps are indeed steep, soulless and forbidding, but they afford a spectacular oblique view of the river, with the grand arches of Key Bridge above and the blue towers of Rosslyn beyond.

Key Bridge is named for **FRANCIS SCOTT KEY** (1779–1843), who composed a poem that was soon being sung to the tune of a British drinking song, "To Anacreon in Heaven." But "The Star Spangled Banner" became our national anthem, by presidential proclamation, only in 1931. Key was a practicing lawyer who served as U. S. attorney for the District of Columbia from 1833 to 1841. During the War of 1812 he went to Baltimore to negotiate the release of a friend being held prisoner on a British ship. The British bombardment of Fort McHenry trapped Key and his friend aboard ship, where they

Key Bridge

remained in an agony of suspense through the long and terrible night. You know the rest of the story.

Key lived at 3518 M Street in a house that was torn down in 1947 to make way for the Whitehurst Freeway access ramp to Key Bridge. The stones were numbered and stored so that the house could be rebuilt in another place, but the National Park Service can't remember where it put them.

The Exorcist Steps will take you down to M Street, but so will 35th Street, which is cobblestoned, steep and charming. On M Street a world of cafes, bistros, bars, trendy eateries and smart shoppes unfolds before you. If you can resist them, get on the towpath that goes along the C & O Canal by proceeding from M down almost any street (except Wisconsin, which will take you where you want to go but not via the towpath.) Follow the towpath to 31st Street, turn right and walk down to the river's edge. Turn left to find restaurants, fountains, statues, action.

An entirely pleasing promenade stretches along the Potomac River from 30th Street to Wisconsin Avenue. One can look down the river to the Watergate and the Kennedy Center, across to Roosevelt Island with its wild trappings of trees and vines, and upriver to that fine Roman aqueduct, Key Bridge. The river itself flows unvexed to the Chesapeake Bay. In good weather it sports jaunty sailboats and eight-oared shells from Georgetown University. When you've seen enough of historic Georgetown, find a place to eat outdoors or just to sit and watch the unfolding scene.

The Georgetown walk takes 1½ to 2 hours.

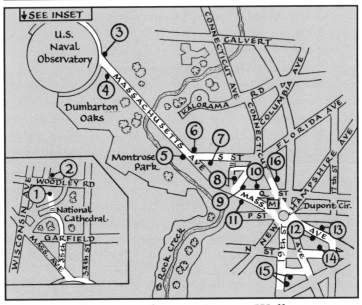

The Massachusetts Avenue Walk

1. The National Cathedral, Wisconsin & Massachusetts Aves.
2. Walter Lippmann: 3525 Woodley Road
3. Kahlil Gibran Memorial Garden
4. Statue of Winston Churchill
5. Edith Hamilton: 2448 Massachusetts Avenue
6. Mary Roberts Rinehart: 2419 Massachusetts Avenue
7. Woodrow Wilson: 2340 S Street
8. Elinor Wylie: 2153 Florida Avenue
9. The Cosmos Club: 2121 Massachusetts Avenue
10. The Phillips Collection: 21st and Q Streets
11. Anderson House: 2118 Massachusetts Avenue
12. Frances Hodgson Burnett: 1770 Massachusetts (site)
13. Henry Cabot Lodge: 1765 Massachusetts (site)
14. Edward Everett Hale: 1741 N Street
15. Theodore Roosevelt: 1820 Jefferson Place and 1215 19th St.
16. Kramerbooks and Afterwords: 1517 Connecticut Avenue

Massachusetts Avenue and Embassy Row

THE MASSACHUSETTS AVENUE WALK BEGINS at the National Cathedral of St. Peter and St. Paul, a full-scale Gothic cathedral that rises heavenward from the highest point in Washington, Mount St. Alban. Here, halfway up the nave on the right, is the fine marble sarcophagus that is the tomb of our perhaps most scholarly president, Woodrow Wilson. The crusader's sword on the tomb commemorates Wilson's valiant battle for peace.

HELEN KELLER (1880–1968) is buried in the cathedral too, as is Anne Sullivan Macy, her teacher and first lifeline to the world. Helen Keller is the author of several books, including *The Story of My Life* (1903) and *Teacher, Anne Sullivan Macy* (1955), which she subtitled "A Tribute from the Foster Child of her Mind." A play, *The Miracle Worker* by William Gibson (1959), also tells of her remarkable triumph over deafness and blindness due to a childhood illness and of Anne Sullivan's equally remarkable role in her life.

Give a nod to the house where Walter Lippmann lived for many years and copiously entertained movers and shakers in his sunken living room at 3525 Woodley Road. Leaving the cathedral by the south doors, enjoy the grounds and gardens of the Cathedral Close, particularly the Bishop's Garden to the right of the steps.

Turn left down the paved road—or follow the wooded walk that begins by the equestrian statue of George Washington, crosses a rustic footbridge and rejoins the paved road—and continue to Garfield Street. Cross Garfield, follow 35th Street to Massachusetts Avenue and go left. The large anchors on the right at 34th Street mark the entrance to the vice-president's house.

On the left you will soon see the new park commemorating Lebanese poet Kahlil Gibran, who wrote *The Prophet*. On the right is the commanding statue of writer-statesman Sir Winston Churchill, who has one foot on British soil and one on American as befits his parentage. Continue down Embassy Row past the Islamic Center (the Mosque) to 2448 Massachusetts Avenue.

For a shorter version of this walk begin at 2448 Massachusetts.

The accomplishments of **EDITH HAMILTON** (1867–1963) are instructive for those thinking they are too old to begin a new career. She was in her sixties when she started writing the books that have made the world of the Greeks and Romans come alive for generations of Americans.

Edith Hamilton's whole life is instructive. She went through Bryn Mawr College in two years, concentrating on the classics, and won a fellowship to study abroad. She chose the University of Munich, where the idea of a woman in the Classics Department was so threatening that the administration suggested she attend classes in a specially built box to avoid the possibility that a seminarian might have to sit next to her, or worse, share a text with her.

She was summoned home by the redoubtable dean of Bryn Mawr College, M. Carey Thomas, to take over the administration of the Bryn Mawr School in Baltimore. A girl's school at its founding in 1885, it was a serious academic institution in a town convinced that a real education would render a girl unmarriageable. One of Baltimore's leading gynecologists told Hamilton that the study of Latin was bad for women's health.

Hamilton made the school preeminent. She opened her students' eyes to the excitement of the intellectual life. In 1930 her first book, *The Greek Way*, was published. To follow were *The Roman Way*, *Mythology*, *Witness to the Truth*, *The Echo of Greece*, and more.

In 1943 she moved to Washington and lived for the remaining twenty years of her life at 2448 Massachusetts Avenue in a pleasant house that backs onto Rock Creek Park. She loved to entertain and moved about like a sandpiper among her guests. Isak Dinesen, Arnold Toynbee, D. T. Suzuki, Robert Frost, Stephen Spender, Robert Lowell, Alexis Léger, John L. Lewis and many others beat a path to her door.

In 1957, in the ancient amphitheater below the Acropolis, she was made an honorary citizen of Athens.

A different cup of tea was **MARY ROBERTS RINEHART** (1876–1958). A doctor's wife and mother of three small boys, she began writing to supplement the family income. In no time at all she found her voice and her audience and became an enormously popular writer of mystery stories. With *The Circular Staircase* in 1908, her reputation entered the stratosphere. A national figure, she became a molder of

2419 Massachusetts Avenue: Mary Roberts Rinehart

middle-class taste and manners through regular contributions to the *Saturday Evening Post*. A *New York Times* poll of 1922 determined that Rinehart was one of the twelve greatest women in America.

She spoke to an audience who, like herself, was shocked by the new realism of writers like Sinclair Lewis. For their part, they did not want to hear about sexuality or anything sordid. She especially didn't want to write like Lewis; there wasn't enough suspense. "Mr. Lewis can take a half dozen pages to get Babbitt out of bed and into the bathroom."

The Rineharts came to Washington from Sewickley, Pennsylvania, in 1922 and moved into the late Senator Boies Penrose's apartment in the Wardman Park (now the Sheraton Washington, 2660 Woodley Road, on the corner of Connecticut Avenue). But Mrs. Rinehart found it unsettling that Penrose's spirit was still there. *The Red Lamp* deals with spirit return, an idea popular at the time.

In 1923 the Rineharts moved into their own fine house, 2419 Massachusetts Avenue (now the Embassy of Zambia), where they remained until Dr. Stanley Rinehart's death in 1932. In 1935 Mrs. Rinehart moved to New York, where her sons had founded the publishing house of Rinehart & Co.

Mary Roberts Rinehart's books had horror and suspense, humor and a buried story, usually a romance. She wrote some twenty books during her time in Washington. The literature department of George Mason University in Fairfax, Virginia, administers the Mary Roberts Rinehart Fund, which assists deserving writers.

Now bear left on S Street.

By the end of World War I, **WOODROW WILSON** (1856–1924) was first citizen of the world, but the stresses and strains attendant on organizing the League of Nations were too much for his health. He suffered a debilitating stroke and was never well again. After leaving 1600 Pennsylvania Avenue, Wilson lived at 2340 S Street, in a red brick Georgian revival townhouse that is preserved much as it was when he lived there. The house is open to the public 9 to 4 every day except Monday.

A scholarly man, his way with words served him well as president and as author of books on politics and history which include a five-volume *History of the American People*. Not everyone admired Wilson. Theodore Roosevelt declared that he used the language "not to communicate his meaning but to conceal it, being fundamentally desirous to cover up his fatal lack of purpose."

Two doors further on is the lovely, small Textile Museum, open 10 to 5 every day except Sunday, when it is open 1 to 5. It's well worth a visit if time permits.

Turn right off S Street onto 22nd Street to the Decatur Terrace steps, known locally as the "Spanish Steps." Go down the steps and turn left on R Street to Florida Avenue. Turn right to 2153 Florida.

2340 S Street: Woodrow Wilson

Elegant, stylish **ELINOR WYLIE** (1885–1928) felt herself spiritually akin to the seventeenth-century metaphysical poets and wrote fastidious, subtle and accomplished verse. She loved delicate, patrician things, fine filagree, mother of pearl, and hummingbird's wings of hammered gold.

Wylie was twelve when her family moved from Philadelphia to 1516 K Street NW. It "had quite a good back garden, climbing roses & honeysuckle & even quite large trees, so it was very open & pleasant." Her teacher sent her a note: "You are unstable as water." Elinor attached it to her mirror. Later the family moved to 1701 Rhode Island Avenue and she attended the Holton Arms School, then on Hillyer Place.

After being introduced to society, as Elinor was, girls were expected to find suitable husbands and embark on their life's work, domesticity. This Elinor Wylie did and soon regretted it. Four years into a stifling marriage, she ran off with Horace Wylie, an older

"The Spanish Steps"

man who had a wife and four children. Washington society was agog. She was a fallen woman; worse, she had betrayed her class.

The lovers fled to Europe. In the course of their ten years together they eventually returned home (to live at 2153 Florida Avenue), married, and grew apart. Or Elinor got bored. They made literary friends: among them Katherine Anne Porter, Sinclair Lewis, who was writing *Main Street*, and Lewis's wife Grace, and William Rose Benét. A small literary clique met at the Wayfarers Bookshop in a basement on H Street, a kind of Washington version of Paris's congenial literary bookstore, Shakespeare and Company. Unable to bear a child, claustrophobic and desperate, Elinor began to write.

Benét encouraged her and helped her get published. *Nets to Catch the Wind* was accepted by Alfred Harcourt, and Bill Benét was in love with her. She would marry him. She left Washington, which had never really forgiven her anyway.

Three more books of poetry appeared and three novels: *Jennifer Lorn, The Venetian Glass Nephew*, her best, and *The Orphan Angel*, an imaginative story about what would have happened if an American ship had saved Shelley from drowning. She was obsessed with Shelley, far more than with the real men in her life. This prompted Sara Teasdale to write, "Elinor Wylie, Elinor Wylie, what do I hear you say? / I wish it were Shelley astride my belly instead of poor Bill Benét."

Pass the Cosmos Club on the corner of Florida and Massachusetts Avenues. This private social club founded in 1878 has had as its members over the years three presidents, two vice-presidents, a dozen supreme court justices, twenty-nine Nobel Prize winners and fifty Pulitzer Prize winners. Its handsome beaux arts building repays a passing glance.

A red brick Georgian revival building on the corner of 21st and Q Streets houses the Phillips Collection, the first permanent museum of modern art in this country, remarkable for its collection and small-scale, private-house setting. Open Monday through Saturday 10 to 5 and Sunday 12 to 7, the elegant and charming ambience of the

Phillips makes the cafe there a good place to break one's journey for lunch or other refreshment.

Across the street is Anderson House, headquarters of the Society of the Cincinnati, an organization founded in 1783 to perpetuate the distinction of the officers of the Revolutionary War and their descendants. Its library specializes in the military history of the Revolution and the period 1750–1800.

What child who has read or heard *The Little Princess* (1888) and *The Secret Garden* (1911) has not been immeasurably enriched by these engaging books? No one could tell a story better or provide more reader satisfaction than **FRANCES HODGSON BURNETT** (1849–1924). In her pages cruel bullies and hardhearted matrons get their comeuppance, disagreeable earls become jolly grandparents, sickly children are made whole among the flowers.

From a grimy childhood in Manchester, England, Frances Hodgson moved with her widowed mother to Tennessee. There at age fifteen she began writing the stories that fairly dripped from her pen for the rest of her life. Marrying the boy across the street, she moved with him to Washington in 1877.

In 1879 they settled in at 1215 I Street. In 1936 David O. Selznick had a plaque put on the door of 1215: "On this site fifty years ago the deathless classic *Little Lord Fauntleroy* was written." The plaque was on the wrong house, the street having been renumbered, but it's all the same now. After a brief phase as an adult bookstore, the house, plaque and all, was razed, as was the real house, two doors away.

Mrs. Hodgson Burnett, known to family and friends as "Fluffy" or "Dearest," was perfectly attuned to the taste of her day. Her books were not children's books; in those days there was no clear line between books for children and books for adults. These were books for everybody. *Little Lord Fauntleroy* (1886), one of the biggest best-sellers of all time, became a cultural phenomenon. Widely serialized, it was made into a play and a movie. There were Fauntleroy playing cards, games, writing paper, toys and chocolates. A less happy spinoff was a war between mothers and sons over velvet suits with trailing sashes, huge Van Dyke collars and lacy cuffs.

In 1883 Burnett wrote a satirical book about Washington called *Through One Administration*.

Her success gave her entree into literary circles, which enthralled her. She entertained lavishly, traveled widely, knew everyone. The grand house she had built at 1770 Massachusetts Avenue is no longer standing.

"She is owed a debt by all introspective children at war with themselves and the world," wrote her biographer Marghanita Laski. Dearest's concern was that everybody should be happy. She, too, was looking for the low door in the wall to the secret garden; in her books she found it.

HENRY CABOT LODGE (1850–1924) may have been a stiff, self-righteous Bostonian, but he could also be charming. A voracious reader and excellent talker with a ready wit, he was never without his thin volume of Shakespeare. Lodge was a scholar and a writer whose *George Washington* was published in 1888, just before the first volume of Theodore Roosevelt's *The Winning of the West*. He lived in a handsome house at 1765 Massachusetts Avenue, where Rudyard Kipling stayed when he came to Washington (the Brookings Institution parking lot occupies the space now).

As Boston Brahmin and senator, Lodge was a player in the Henry Adams-John Hay crowd, perhaps to his regret when Hay and his wife Nannie—she of the violet eyes—fell in love. The Adams crowd included the Hays and geologist-entrepreneur Clarence King, Senator and Mrs. Donald Cameron (the beauteous Lizzie), the painter John La Farge, the Lodges, Theodore Roosevelt and a few select others. Breakfast at Henry Adams's was a regular event. No one was actually invited, but all knew who would be welcome.

Roosevelt and Henry Cabot Lodge had one of the great friendships in American political history. When TR first came to Washington he stayed with the Lodges. Later he moved to 1820 Jefferson Place, and then to 1215 19th Street.

Roosevelt was not a fan of Woodrow Wilson. "I despise the man and dislike his policies." Wilson was "an infernal skunk," "an abject coward," "an utterly insincere hypocrite" (the worst kind) and "a Byzantine logothete." He didn't like him.

At fifty grips a minute, **THEODORE ROOSEVELT** (1859–1919) may have been not only the fastest handshaker in history but also one of the most democratic. He made his hand available to all who were sober, washed and "free of bodily advertising."

TR was a human juggernaut, a bundle of unbounded energy and enthusiasm, rushing through life like an express train. "Dee-lighted," he would cry, throwing himself into the moment. He was, in the words of one of his children, "the bride at every wedding, and the corpse at every funeral."

"Over or through, never around," was his rule for a pleasurable point-to-point walk with friends. In a letter to his son Kermit in 1908 he describes such a walk in Rock Creek Park: "The ice had just broken and the creek was a swollen flood, running like a millrace. We did the usual climbing stunts at the various rocks, and then swam the creek; and it was a good swim, in our winter clothes and with hobnailed boots and the icy current running really fast." Did his friends find this as pleasurable as he did? One wonders.

He wrote well and had an intellectual range well beyond his clear predelictions for history and nature. His collected letters to his children, whom he adored, became a bestseller. *The Winning of the West* (four volumes, 1889–1896), is a first-class account of U. S. expansion after the Civil War. TR was a staunch believer in Americanism and abhorred those who didn't flock to its banner, like that "miserable little snob" Henry James.

In 1895 Rudyard Kipling visited Washington and the two men got on well enough. He liked to drop in at the Cosmos Club (then on Lafayette Square) about ten-thirty in the evening, the hour when TR was likely to be there pronouncing "definitive opinions on every mote in the cosmos."

Roosevelt Island, in a setting appropriately wild, has a fine rugged memorial to Theodore Roosevelt. A large statue of him stands in a clearing surrounded by granite tablets on which the beliefs he lived by are engraved.

EDWARD EVERETT HALE (1822–1909) wrote several books, including memoirs and *Franklin in France*, a lively account of Benjamin Franklin's years as our ambassador in Paris. But he is best remembered for his short story, "The Man without a Country." Hale, a Unitarian minister, was chaplain of the Senate from 1903 to 1909. He was asked, "Dr. Hale, do you pray for the Senate?" "No," replied Hale. "I look at the Senate and pray for the people." Hale lived at 1741 N Street, now part of the Tabard Inn.

Consider having lunch at Kramerbooks and Afterwords, a bookstore-cum-eatery at 1517 Connecticut Avenue, just north of Dupont Circle. Good ambience, good food, Bloomsday readings on June 16.

Dupont Circle

Further up Connecticut Avenue at the Wardman Park (too far for this walk), **CLARE BOOTHE LUCE** (1903–1987) was unaware of the spirits Mary Roberts Rinehart had felt. Luce was a paradigm of midcentury American womanhood. Using her brains and her sex purposefully, she may have missed some of life's opportunities, but she didn't miss many.

After an early first marriage to a rich man, she married Henry Luce, founder of what became Time-Life, Inc., a man with a mission as well as a fortune. Though her husband's publishing empire viewed her with apprehension, it was she who provided the idea for a large-format pictorial newsmagazine. *Life* was her brainchild.

As a young woman Clare Boothe had flirted with the idea of an acting career, but she really wanted to write. In 1929 she went to *Vogue* to ask its editor, Edna Woolman Chase, for a job, but Mrs. Chase was in Europe. Rather than wait for her return, Clare walked directly into an editorial office, sat down at an empty desk, and asked for an assignment. They gave her one; she was to write picture captions for a feature article on the well-dressed woman. All went well until payday when it was noticed that there was no check for Clare.

Eventually she got on the payroll at *Vogue* but after a few months set her sights on writing for Frank Crowninshield's *Vanity Fair*. With her contacts and, more importantly, her flair for satire, which was *Vanity Fair's* strong suit, she landed a job. It was 1930. She married Henry Luce in 1935. In 1936 her best-known play, *The Women*, opened on Broadway and ran for a year and a half. It satirized rich, bitchy American women; she got the idea from a conversation overheard in a ladies' room. *Kiss the Boys Goodbye* (1938), *Margin for Error* (1939), and other plays followed. Uniquely positioned as she was, assertive and talented, she became a correspondent for Life, covering the early years of World War II in the Far East and North Africa.

Clare Boothe Luce was elected to Congress from Connecticut in 1943; she served two terms. Told she had the best legs in Washington, she said she wanted to be known for her other end. She was a celebrity at large, a world-class glamour girl, a force. It didn't hurt that she was, as Cecil Beaton said, "drenchingly beautiful."

From 1953 to 1956 she was U.S. ambassador to Rome. The Italians were appalled that we had sent a woman.

After Henry Luce's death in 1967, with the power and the parties receding, she moved back to Washington from Hawaii to live at the Watergate, where she had a magnificent view up the river to Key Bridge and the spires of Georgetown University.

The Massachusetts Avenue walk (long version) takes 1½ to 2 hours; the shorter version, 1 hour.

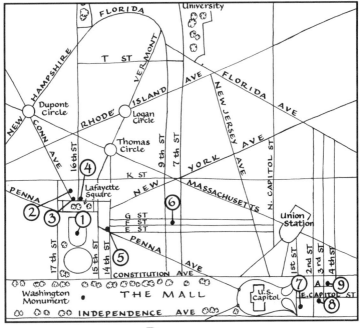

Downtown

1. The White House, 1600 Pennsylvania Avenue
2. Site of the Daniel Webster house, now the Chamber of Commerce, H and Connecticut
3. The Hay-Adams Hotel
4. St. John's Church
5. The Willard Hotel, 14th and Pennsylvania
6. National Portrait Gallery/Museum of American Art (formerly the Patent Office)
7. Library of Congress
8. Folger Shakespeare Library, 201 E. Capitol Street
9. Frederick Douglass Museum, 318 A Street

From the White House
to the Capitol

THERE AT THE very beginning, **ANNE ROYALL** (1769–1854) was one of the first women writers on national affairs and the first Washington muckraker, columnist and commentator. She is credited with inventing the quoted interview. Born when George III ruled the colonies, she lived to see the rise of Abraham Lincoln and interviewed him and every president before him.

From her base in Washington she traveled around the country by stagecoach, collecting material for *Sketches of History, Life, and Manners in the United States* (1826) and for her newspapers (she founded two: *Paul Pry* in 1831 and *The Huntress* in 1836). Often destitute, she lived sometimes by begging, sometimes by blackmail, always by her wits.

Her pieces were full of gossip, politics and diatribes against the church. Her tongue was shrill and fearless. She exposed graft and incompetence wherever she found it and railed at congressmen, who fled when they saw her coming. "I can fathom their rascality," she said. Her mobcap with wispy grey hair escaping from it was a familiar sight all over Washington. She narrowly escaped a ducking in the Potomac and did not escape a ten-dollar fine when she was tried as a "common scold" in a federal court.

Her causes were separation of church and state, sound money, justice to the Indians, free thought, free speech, free press, public schools free from religious bias, liberal appropriations for scientific investigation and good works instead of long prayers.

John Quincy Adams wrote in his diary: "Mrs. Royall . . . continues to make herself noxious to many persons." She was reputed to have stood by his clothes as he swam in the Potomac so that he would have to talk to her.

She lived in rooms and boarding houses, always in the shadow of the Capitol. On these sites now exist the Library of Congress and the Supreme Court.

She was buried in an unmarked grave in Congressional Cemetery, 1801 E Street SE. But she was not entirely forgotten. Some fifty years later a small plaque was placed on the grave. It read: "Anne Royall, Pioneer Woman Publicist, 1769–1854. 'I Pray That The Union Of These States May Be Eternal.' "

DANIEL WEBSTER (1782–1852) asked **WASHINGTON IRVING** (1783–1859) to bring Charles Dickens to dine. Webster's dinner invitations were always oral. This one went: "I have, Sir, purchased in market this morning a famous opossum. I have sent it to Monica, my cook, to prepare it in true Virginia fashion, stuffed with chestnuts and baked with sweet potatoes. It will be a dish fit for the gods. Come, Sir, and try it."

Webster lived in a grand mansion on the northeast corner of H and Connecticut, present site of the U.S. Chamber of Commerce, where Webster's desk may still be seen. A legendary orator and advocate, he inspired Stephen Vincent Benét's *The Devil and Daniel Webster*. A statue of him stands at Scott Circle.

Author of books on American history and influential patron of the arts, Webster supported and encouraged many writers of the early nineteenth century. He was able to get Washington Irving appointed minister to Spain, a country that Irving had fallen in love with and that had inspired four of his books, including *The Legends of the Alhambra*. Irving, in his role of man of letters and mentor of visiting writers, often came to Washington. It was Washington Irving who urged Dickens to visit this country.

In 1842, when he was thirty years old, **CHARLES DICKENS** (1812–1870) was enormously popular in England and perhaps even more widely adored here, where his admirers mobbed him. Dickens's impressions of us, which eventually appeared as *American Notes*, were less flattering. He found Washington "bilious." Indeed, what made the biggest impression on him was the spitting habits of American men. "Washington is the headquarters of tobacco-tinctured saliva." "The thing itself is an exaggeration of nastiness, which cannot be outdone." On the train, "the flashes of saliva flew so perpetually and incessantly out of the windows all the way it looked as though they were ripping open feather beds inside and letting the wind dispose of the feathers. . . . And in every bar-room and hotel passage the stone floor looks as if it were paved with open oysters."

In 1868 he came back, older and in need of money. Reading Little Nell's death scene, he entranced audiences, who stood and applauded with tears streaming down their faces until he returned to the stage.

He visited President Andrew Johnson, who told him about Lincoln's dream before the assassination. Dickens was struck by it, almost obsessed, telling and retelling it.

Lincoln lay in a small bedroom off the room in which Mary slept in a huge carved bed. He dreamed that he awakened to an unnaturally still house. He hears subdued sobbing. No one is about; the beds are empty. He wanders downstairs. The hall is empty, but still unseen mourners continue to sob. The East Room is crowded with people. There on a catafalque covered with black velvet lies a body, the face covered with a cloth. Grim-faced mourners file past, some weeping, some gazing dolefully at the corpse. "Who is dead in the White House?" he asks a guard.

"The president," says the soldier. "He was killed by an assassin."

Lincoln awoke, covered with sweat. What does it mean, he wondered? Will this happen? Do dreams predict the future?

Lincoln had a great interest in omens, premonitions and the significance of dreams, and so did Dickens. The novelist was drawn to the ambiguous gray area between foreshadowing and clairvoyance. What, he wondered, can we ward off, and how?

Lincoln, a man of great subtlety, used language with the deftness and elegance of a dancing master: "The dogmas of the quiet past are inadequate to the stormy present. The occasion is piled high with difficulty, and we must rise with the occasion. As our case is new, so we must think anew and act anew. We must disenthrall ourselves, and then we shall save our country." He worked at his prose to make it spare. His speech may have been plain, but it was never artless.

MARGARET LEECH (1893–1974) was as moved by the Civil War as we still are, and she makes that time come alive in *Reveille in Washington*, a book that is a treat indeed.

"Burnside stood beside the President on the balcony of Willard's, reviewing the troops. Whitman stood on the corner with his new friend John Burroughs. Soldiers waved and called him by name. The redbud was in flower along Rock Creek."

Leech began her exhaustive research at the Library of Congress in 1935. She combed through old photographs, newspapers, letters, documents and personal accounts, immersing herself in the Washington of the early 1860s. The haunting, still-photograph quality of dispirited men leaning on muskets, the randomness of death in the gentle Virginia fields—no one has more effectively caught the immediacy of the war from the battlefields to the drawing rooms of Washington. *Reveille* won the Pulitzer Prize for history in 1942.

Of disparate heroes of the time, Leech wrote, "While the blond war god, Hooker, rode out on his milk-white horse, and the heart of the Union rose again with the rise of a new hero, a big, blowzy fellow in a grey suit was beginning to be known in the streets and hospital wards of Washington." WALT WHITMAN (1819–1892) came to Washington in 1862 to nurse his brother George, who had been wounded at Fredericksburg, the battle that gave Louisa May Alcott, nursing in a different hospital, her first Civil War patients.

Washington and its environs were one vast hospital. Whitman, already the poet of *Leaves of Grass*, lived in a room at 1407 L Street NW, for which he paid $7 a month, and also at 1205 M Street (neither residence remains). He found George in stable condition, but there was plenty of work for a hospital volunteer to do.

Whitman believed in the curative powers of affection. He made himself useful changing dressings, writing letters for the soldiers, playing twenty questions with them, cheering them up with little offerings of tobacco, an apple or a book. He cared about them, and they responded in kind. Out of his war experience came parts of *Specimen Days* and *Drum Taps*. But the war profoundly affected him in ways he couldn't address, and twelve years had to pass before he was able to publish *Memoranda during the War*. "The interior history of the war will never be written," he said, "perhaps must not and should not be." It was too horrible, too powerful and moving an experience to be violated by the telling. "The real war will never get in the books."

After the war, Whitman worked as a clerk in the Indian Bureau of the Department of the Interior, which was housed in the basement of that shrine to American ingenuity, the Patent Office (now the National Portrait Gallery and the Museum of American Art, 9th Street between G and F). The building warehoused the wounded during the war and later was the site of Lincoln's Second Inaugural Ball. When the secretary of the interior found a copy of *Leaves of Grass* in a drawer, he read it with horror and fired its author. Outraged, his friends got him transferred to the attorney general's office, and he remained in Washington until poor health forced him to leave in 1873.

Though an exuberant patriot, Whitman was not unaware of his country's failings. In the era of unabashed avarice after the war known as the Gilded Age, he decried the "deep disease" of American society and politics. "Our New World democracy . . . is, so far, an almost complete failure in its social aspects, and in really grand religious, moral, literary and aesthetic results." He wrote of presidential candidates Fillmore and Pierce, "Never were publicly displayed more deformed, mediocre, snivelling, unreliable, false-hearted men." Before he was aware of Abraham Lincoln, he prefigured him, calling for a "Redeemer President" to come from "the real west, the log hut, the clearing, the woods, the prairie."

Sonorous, cadenced, wide-visioned Whitman. He heard America singing, and eventually America heard him back. "Stop this day and night with me and you shall possess the origin of all poems," he wrote.

BRUCE CATTON (1899–1978), journalist and historian, became director of information for the War Production Board in 1942. Out of this Washington experience came *War Lords of Washington*. He didn't start to publish his monumental and moving books about the Civil War until after he left government service. *A Stillness at Appomattox* won the Pulitzer Prize and the National Book Award in 1953. While in Washington he lived at 3139 Tennyson Street NW.

Lafayette Square was a handsome and vital place in the second half of the nineteenth century. It mostly still is, but don't go there at night. To the south lies Pennsylvania Avenue and the White House; to the north H Street, with the gold-topped steeple of St. John's (the church of the presidents) in one corner. On Madison Place to the east and Jackson Place to the west stand grand federal houses that have seen a lot of history. Stephen Decatur, Daniel Webster, Henry Clay, John C. Calhoun and Dolley Madison, among others, have lived on the square.

It was here to the house at 1607 H Street that Mr. and Mrs. Henry Adams moved in 1880. **HENRY ADAMS** (1838–1918), grandson and great-grandson of presidents, was a historian, a man of letters and an arbiter of taste. He and his wife Clover, a sharp-witted intellectual whom Henry James called a "Voltaire in petticoats," knew all the right people, went to their houses, entertained them at their own.

The discriminating Adamses had perhaps too fine a filtering system for the vulgarities of the world. Sometimes they suffered from what they feared most, ennui. Or worse, they failed to be amused. But at other times their life seemed quite idyllic: horseback riding in Rock Creek Park, dining at the White House (until even it became too vulgar for them), a life at the center of things. Their sunny drawing room, with its tall windows giving onto the park, was the most exclusive and lively salon in Washington.

Henry Adams produced biographies, two novels, *Esther* and *Democracy*, a nine-volume *History of the United States During the Administrations of Thomas Jefferson and James Madison*, a classic book on art, *Mont-Saint-Michel and Chartres* (1904) and an outstanding autobiography, *The Education of Henry Adams*, which was published after his death and won him a Pulitzer Prize. His novel, *Democracy*, is highly readable, amusing, and strangely relevant to social and political Washington today.

Adams and **JOHN HAY** (1838–1905) engaged Henry Hobson Richardson, the country's most distinguished architect, to design adjoining houses for them. Adams's house at 1603 H Street faced across Lafayette Square to the White House. Hay's house fronted on 16th Street and looked at St. John's Church. These handsome and important houses were torn down in the 1920s and replaced with the Hay-Adams Hotel. The arches of the Adams house were saved and installed in a house then going up at 2618 31st Street NW, where, strangely evocative, they remain today.

Hay, also a writer, was co-author of a life of Abraham Lincoln and anonymously published a novel, *The Bread-Winners*. Hay was Lincoln's private secretary, secretary of state, ambassador to England and a good man to know.

When Clover Adams killed herself in 1885, Henry, who never fully understood why she did it and never mentioned it, commissioned the most famous sculptor of the day, Augustus Saint-Gaudens, to make a statue for her grave in Rock Creek Cemetery (Rock Creek Church Road and Webster Street NW.) Equally famous architect Stanford White designed the setting. Though Saint-Gaudens was asked to create a figure expressing acceptance of the inevitable, the statue was given the name "Grief." In fact, the name is not quite accurate and certainly not the whole story. Neither male nor female, open to many interpretations, the figure is nothing if not ambiguous—silently expressing something profound but impalpable. (See Washington author Burke Wilkinson's *Uncommon Clay, The Life and Works of Augustus Saint-Gaudens* for more about this.)

Henry Adams lived on, traveling, writing, even falling in love, but a golden time had ended. The well-ordered society he had known was breaking down. In its place a new breed of brash and ostentatious men holding the new wealth of the industrial revolution was coming to power.

When Adams died in 1918, he joined Clover in Rock Creek Cemetery and perhaps also at what Hay once called "the ghost-haunted corner of 16th and H."

The Adams Memorial,
Rock Creek Park

In 1882 OSCAR WILDE (1854–1900) and HENRY JAMES (1843–1916) visited the city at the same time. James was here to see his friends the Henry Adamses. Looking down his nose a bit, he pronounced Washington "the democratic equivalent of a court city," and the Capitol not unlike a railway station, with "a crowd of shabby people circulating in a labyrinth of spittoons."

Wilde's reasons for coming had to do with his need for cash, and he wanted to bring aestheticism to America, to convert the philistines. Going through customs, he is reputed to have told the officials, "I have nothing to declare except my genius."

As a matter of courtesy James called on Wilde at his hotel. James, who lived in England, remarked that he was nostalgic for London. "Really!" sniffed Wilde. "You care for *places*? The *world* is my home." James pronounced him "a fatuous fool, tenth-rate cad," and "an unclean beast."

Wilde wore a languishing look, and his clothes were often purposefully cobwebby, "with a tender bloom like cold gravy." He sighed that he despaired of living up to his blue china. He was good copy and the press had a field day. "In old days," said Wilde, "men had the rack; now they have the press."

Wilde had a sense of what would amuse and amusingly outrage, and he captivated most of Washington. He beguiled Frances Hodgson Burnett by telling her that art critic John Ruskin considered her a true artist. She in turn introduced him to other writers. He attended one of her receptions (when she was living on I Street) attired in a black silk claw-hammer coat, a flowered waistcoat, knee breeches, silk stockings (to show off his shapely calves) and patent leather shoes with large buckles (to set off his very small feet). The excesses of Wilde's aestheticism created the climate for a Fauntleroy; he was himself a Fauntleroy prototype. Wilde was the author of a novel, *The Picture of Dorian Gray* (1891), many witty plays including *The Importance of Being Earnest* and *Lady Windermere's Fan*, poems and fairy tales.

A more rugged fellow was **BRET HARTE** (1836–1902), circa 1870 the most popular writer in America. His was the voice of the frontier experience—a big voice with an even bigger market. Leaving New York for California at the age of nineteen, Harte mined gold, taught school and practiced journalism. He was enormously successful as editor of the *Overland Monthly,* to which he contributed his own stories. In those stories, including his best-known "The Luck of Roaring Camp" and "The Outcasts of Poker Flat," Harte created the western stereotype we know and love today. These first formula westerns featured the diamond-in-the-rough hero, the kindly thief, the good-hearted whore and a supporting caste of assorted hombres and deadbeats.

Mark Twain, who first met him in San Francisco, considered Harte a deadbeat and a rogue. Their paths crossed often. Twain elaborated: Harte was a liar, thief, swindler, snob, sot, sponge and coward.

But others found him a pleasant companion and a witty conversationalist. In the beginning things went well for Harte. He followed up on the success of his stories with a humorous poem entitled "Plain Language from Truthful James," otherwise known as "Ah Sin" or "The Heathen Chinee."

He came back east to collaborate with Mark Twain (an interesting alliance), on a musical version of "Ah Sin." It played at the National Theater in Washington to modest applause, then went to New York, where it died.

Harte stayed on in Washington having a bad time. Living at the Rigg's Hotel, 1617 I Street, he made it through what he called "that awful, terrible winter" of 1877–78 sustained by his friendship with John Hay. Ubiquitous Hay got Harte a job as consul in Crefeld, Germany, to which he departed in 1878 never to return.

MARK TWAIN (1835–1910) was in and out of Washington, always hustling. In 1867 he served briefly as secretary to Senator William Stewart of Nevada, whom he had met in the West. Twain devoted most of his time to writing for various newspapers and soon became disillusioned with government corruption: "There is no distinctively native criminal class except Congress."

Twain saw the comedy in life, but underneath he was not an optimistic man and he questioned whether the American experiment was, in fact, a success. He wrote about his experience in "Washington in 1868." *The Gilded Age*, written with Charles Dudley Warner, also skewers the squalid greed and puffery of Washington and elsewhere. "It's all about money," he wrote. "Money is God—Gold and greenbacks and stock, father, son and the ghost of same."

Twain lived briefly in a house that stood at 14th and F Streets NW, but he took his meals where the action was—at Willard's Hotel.

In the nineteenth century much of the business of Washington was done at Willard's Hotel (now the Willard, 14th and Pennsylvania Avenue NW). The lobby, according to historian Margaret Leech, was

The Willard Hotel

full of the same sallow, determined men, dressy ladies and screaming children as hotels all over America. Huge meals were served at every opportunity to throngs of dignitaries. Conversation was conducted through a haze of blue smoke. In the spring guests feasted on shad and strawberries.

Walt Whitman wrote a poem about the bar in the Willard, and Lincoln stayed there before his inauguration. Julia Ward Howe attended a massive military review with President Lincoln and others in late 1861. Such an impressive spectacle was it that she went back to her room at the Willard and wrote "The Battle Hymn of the Republic." The Pennsylvania Avenue side of the hotel bears a plaque commemorating her.

Novelist **NATHANIEL HAWTHORNE** (1804–1864) stayed at the Willard when he was covering the Civil War for the *Atlantic Monthly*. Charles Dickens stayed there on both visits to Washington. Members of Congress stayed there in the days before they brought their wives and families to the capital with them. In the pre-Civil War period unionists and secessionists used different entrances and stayed on different floors of the hotel.

The Willard has always been the crown jewel of Washington hotels, the "hotel of the presidents." The current structure, an impressive beaux arts building built in 1901, has been faithfully restored to its turn-of-the-century grandeur.

In April 1854 poet **EMILY DICKINSON** (1830–1886), her mother, sister and brother stayed at the Willard while visiting Emily's father, then a congressman from Amherst, Massachusetts. They visited Mount Vernon. She wrote a friend "how one soft spring day we glided down the Potomac in a painted boat, and jumped upon the shore—how hand in hand we stole along up a tangled pathway till we reached the tomb of General George Washington. . . . Thank the Ones in Light that he has at last passed in through a brighter wicket! Oh, I could spend a long day, if it did not weary you, telling of Mount Vernon."

A two-fisted drinker, **AMBROSE BIERCE** (1842–1914?) was a strikingly handsome man with piercing blue eyes and an erect carriage whose reputation for evil made him irresistible to the ladies. His mordant view of life was deeply felt. He served with distinction in the Civil War and his war stories, strange and somber, are full of savage realism and unremitting horror.

Bierce first came to Washington in 1886. In 1900 as correspondent for the Hearst newspapers, he returned to live at 603 15th Street. He was then at the height of his powers as a witty and crusading muckraker. "To hate rascality is my religion." He had published *In the Midst of Life* and *Can Such Things Be?* and was still to write *The Devil's Dictionary*.

Bierce stayed in Washington ten years, living at the Olympia Apartments, 14th and Euclid Streets NW. In the fall of 1913, a wreck from alcohol and asthma, he left for Mexico. "Why should I remain in a country that is on the brink of women's suffrage and prohibition?" he asked. Somehow he got credentials to travel as an observer with the revolutionary army of General Pancho Villa. Nothing more was ever heard from or about him.

Earlier he had written, "If you should hear of my being stood up against a Mexican stone wall and shot to rags, please know that I think it is a pretty good way to depart this life. It beats old age, disease or falling down the cellar stairs. To be a Gringo in Mexico, ah, that is euthanasia."

In the movie made from the novel *The Old Gringo* by Carlos Fuentes, Gregory Peck was Bierce, who, after a last poignant romance with the character played by Jane Fonda, ended up at the stone wall.

An even more colorful character was the flamboyant poet Cincinnatus Miller, who called himself **JOAQUIN MILLER** (1837–1913), shedding a heavy classical name for that of a Mexican bandit. It was more his style.

After an adventurous existence in the Northwest, living with Indians, mining for gold, establishing a pony express route and acquiring the western persona that would stand him in good stead, he went to live in England in 1870. There his volume of poems, *Songs of the Sierras* (1871), was well received, and the man himself was a big hit trading as the embodiment of the Wild West.

In boots and sombrero, an overcoat buttoned with gold nuggets, a bearskin flung over his shoulder, he cut a fine figure. Lest interest in him flag, he smoked three cigars at once, galloped around the dinner table on all fours, bit the ankles of debutantes and swallowed goldfish.

In 1885 he returned to the United States and built a handhewn log cabin at 16th and Crescent Place NW, now Meridian Hill Park. Washington, too, took kindly to him, but he was unable to find high office as he had hoped. Perhaps it was the sombrero.

In 1912 the Miller cabin was moved from Meridian Hill to its present location at picnic area No. 6 on Beach Drive near the intersection of Military Road in Rock Creek Park. It is used, appropriately, for poetry readings in the summer.

Chapters, A Literary Bookstore, at 1512 K Street NW, is another oasis in the city. It offers readings and other literary to-dos as well as richly stocked shelves.

It was Frances Hodgson Burnett's husband, the great Dr. Swann Burnett, who operated on and saved the remaining eye of **JAMES THURBER** (1894–1961) the first having been put out by an arrow shot by his brother when they were boys. The Thurbers were spending the summer in Falls Church, Virginia, at 319 Maple Avenue, now called James Thurber Court. Thurber's contributions to American humor were many, from *Is Sex Necessary?* (with E. B. White), 1929, up through *The Thurber Carnival* in 1945 and *The Thirteen Clocks* in 1950. The name of Walter Mitty, his mild-mannered man with big fantasies, has entered the language.

The Thurbers also lived in town at 2031 I Street NW, not far from 1717 I Street, where **WILLIAM ROSE BENET** (1886–1950) and Laura Benét lived as children. **STEPHEN VINCENT BENET** (1898–1943) was yet to be born. Later Stephen Benét and Thurber were to work together in the code room of the State Department.

Stephen Vincent Benét wrote powerful folk ballads based on American history. *John Brown's Body* is stirring, with its feel for countrysides and racial skeins and the people's talk and song. It won a Pulitzer Prize in 1929. His short story "The Devil and Daniel Webster" was made into an opera, a play and a film.

William Rose Benét was a prolific poet who also wrote a novel in verse, *Rip Tide* (1932), and a Pulitzer Prize-winning verse autobiography, *The Dust Which Is God* (1941). His *Reader's Encyclopedia* is an English major's best friend.

Consider the Library of Congress. Adjacent to the U. S. Capitol, this exemplary monument to civilization, the largest library in the world, collects and safeguards products of the human intellect in buildings that bespeak grandeur. The main entrance hall of the Jefferson Building taxes one's ability to absorb opulence and splendor.

The library has become a national cultural center. It offers concerts, exhibitions, poetry and prose readings, lectures, films and publications. The card file in the main reading room holds twenty-five million cards.

The Chair of Poetry in the English Language (whose occupant has been called Consultant in Poetry and, since 1986, Poet Laureate) was the idea of the eighth librarian of Congress, Herbert Putnam, and was endowed by Archer Huntington (railroad money) in 1936. Now funded by a bequest from benefactor of the arts Gertrude Clark Whittall, the job varies somewhat with the imagination and energy of the incumbent. Conrad Aiken said of the position, "It was not exactly fictitious, but shall we say slightly imaginary." Karl Shapiro recalled (in the third person), "What he liked best was the brushing of elbows, the slight looks and exchanges of the poets who were great, who were held in awe by the world." Reed Whittemore called it a catbird seat.

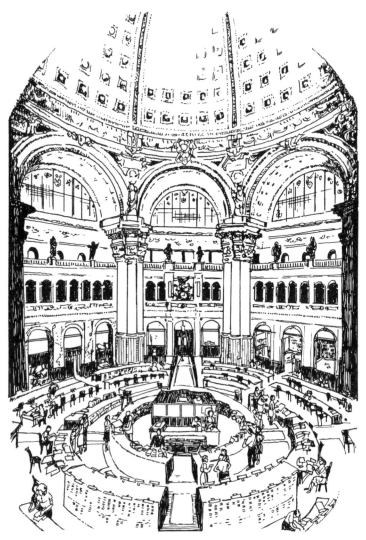

Reading room, Library of Congress

The occupants of the Chair of Poetry have been: Joseph Auslander (1937–41), Allen Tate (1943–44), Robert Penn Warren (1944–45), Louise Bogan (1945–46), Karl Shapiro (1946–47), Robert Lowell (1948–49), Leonie Adams (1948–49), Elizabeth Bishop (1949–50), Conrad Aiken (1950–52), William Carlos Williams (appointed but did not serve), Randall Jarrell (1956–58), Robert Frost (1958–59), Richard Eberhart (1959–61), Louis Untermeyer (1961–63), Howard Nemerov (1963–64), Stephen Spender (1965–66), James Dickey (1966–68), William Jay Smith (1968–70), William Stafford (1970–71), Josephine Jacobsen (1971–73), Daniel Hoffman (1973–74), Stanley Kunitz (1974–76), Robert Hayden (1976–78), William Meredith (1978–80), Maxine Kumin (1980–82), Anthony Hecht (1982–84), Robert Fitzgerald (appointed but did not serve), Reed Whittemore, interim consultant (1984–85) Gwendolyn Brooks (1985–86), Robert Penn Warren again (1986–87), Richard Wilbur (1987–88), Howard Nemerov (1988–90), Mark Strand (1990–91), Joseph Brodsky (1991–92), Mona Van Duyn (1992–93), Rita Dove (1993–   ).

Around the corner from the Library of Congress is the Folger Shakespeare Library, 201 E. Capitol Street. Well-known writers of fiction give readings here in the charming little Elizabethan theater under the auspices of the PEN/Faulkner Program. The Folger poetry program similarly offers readings by contemporary poets.

Nearby, at 318 A Street NE, stands the house in which Frederick Douglass lived before he moved to Cedar Hill. Read more about Douglass in the last chapter, Further Afield.

1934 4th Street: Paul Laurence Dunbar

Seventh Street
and Howard University

PAUL LAURENCE DUNBAR (1872–1906), the first black American poet to achieve an international reputation, was one of the best-known poets in America at the turn of the century.

Although he showed great promise in high school in Ohio, the only job he could find after graduation was as an elevator operator. *Lyrics of Lowly Life* (1896) established Dunbar as the first African-American poet of national reputation since Phillis Wheatley (1753?–1784). He came to Washington in 1887, worked at the Library of Congress (bringing books out from the stacks) and lived in Le Droit Park at 1934 4th Street NW. After he married Alice Moore, whose picture he had seen in a newspaper, they lived at 321 U Street. Dunbar found in Le Droit Park a cohesive and self-sufficient black community, and he was happy there.

In his poetry Dunbar successfully used black themes and dialect, but the writers of the Harlem Renaissance later repudiated him for conforming to white standards. His promising career was cut short when he died of tuberculosis at the age of thirty-four.

Molder and mentor of talents, the original, elite Dunbar High School at 1st and N Streets NW, built in 1916 and torn down in 1977, was for years his memorial. A new Dunbar High stands almost on the same spot.

In Washington from World War I through the depression, Seventh Street was "soul" street. Waves of immigrants from the rural south provided ever larger infusions of personality and inventiveness. Lively, raucous, vibrant, Seventh Street was lined with pool halls, flophouses, barbershops, storefront churches, pawnshops and eateries featuring southern home cooking.

Twice daily enormous crowds poured out of the Howard Theater around the corner at 624 T Street. The Howard was to Washington what the Apollo was to Harlem, a shrine to black musical and comedy genius. All the big names came through the Howard, playing to glorious crowds. After the theater let out, the beat went on late into the night at the Dreamland, the Old Rose Social Club and the Off-Beat.

Artistically, Seventh Street and its environs fell victim to integration. When there was no longer a reason for a black creative enclave, black talent went to other stages. The Howard Theater still stands, but its melancholy condition barely hints at the commanding Italian Renaissance building it once was. As for Seventh Street itself, burned in the 1968 riots, it takes even more imagination to conjure up its vitality of another day. (The historical and artistic life of the Seventh Street area is described in detail in *The Guide to Black Washington* by Sandra Fitzpatrick and Maria R. Goodwin.)

The Harlem Renaissance, a brief but glittering movement in the 1920s, witnessed an exuberant flowering of African-American talent. White America became interested in black culture, music and art as never before. It was new, it was exciting and most of all it was liberating. Largely in New York, but also in Washington, Detroit and Chicago, African-American creative genius was catching fire.

Seventh Street in its heyday influenced three of the brightest stars of the Harlem Renaissance before they moved on to New York. ZORA NEALE HURSTON (1891–1960), talented and high-spirited, refused to take herself or anything else too seriously. A major player in the Harlem Renaissance, she knew everyone on the creative scene, referring to herself and her peers as the "niggerati."

Hurston was an enigmatic figure. Supporting herself as a manicurist, waitress (at the Cosmos Club), librarian, teacher, folklorist, maid and writer, mostly she was a writer. She came north from Florida to Washington and from 1919 to 1924 was part of the exuberant cultural life at Howard University. From Howard she went to Barnard (the only black girl in the class), and then to Columbia Graduate School, where she fell under the spell of the great anthropologist Franz Boas. Hurston researched cultural anthropology—specifically Negro folklore—not just to further her studies but to provide material for her fiction.

Her best-known novel, *Their Eyes Were Watching God* (1937), is deservedly popular. In addition, she wrote two books of folklore— the best-known is *Mules and Men* (1935)—two other novels, short stories and an autobiography, *Dust Tracks on a Road* (1942). The public loved them.

Toward the end of her life she became friendly with Marjorie Kinnan Rawlings who introduced her to the great editor Maxwell Perkins. Perkins advanced money to Hurston to enable her to continue writing and no doubt would have advanced more had he not died in 1947. Sadly, she fell on hard times and had to find work as a maid in Miami. This bright star, this gifted and witty woman, died impoverished and alone.

JEAN TOOMER (1894–1967) was born in Washington, where his family was part of the black aristocracy. He lived at 1341 U Street with his uncle Pinckney B. S. Pinchback, who at the time was the only African-American to have served as acting governor of a state (Louisiana) and was twice denied a seat in the U.S. Senate because of allegedly fraudulent elections. On U Street in 1923 Toomer wrote his novel *Cane*, considered to be the literary jewel of the Harlem Renaissance.

Cane is composed of poems and short stories arranged in a circular pattern, from rural south to urban north and back again. As Cain, it also referred to the Gothic quality of southern history and the ambivalence of those who toiled in the earth and at the same time derived from it a kind of spiritual nourishment. The novel ranked Jean Toomer as a major black writer with Ralph Ellison and Richard Wright.

Toomer became interested in the teachings of the Greek spiritual philosopher Gurdjieff and then in the Quaker religion. When he stopped searching for further answers, his creativity dried up.

Raised by his grandmother, **LANGSTON HUGHES** (1902–1967) had lived in six American cities by the time he was twelve. He worked as a truck farmer, cook, waiter, sailor and doorman at a Paris nightclub before he came to visit his mother in Washington in 1925 while waiting for a scholarship to Lincoln University in Oxford, Pennsylvania. His uncle was former acting president and dean of the law school at Howard University. This placed Hughes squarely in the black upper class, which wasn't where he wanted to be. Scornful of the genteel attitudes of what he called "cultured colored society," he immersed himself in mass culture and tried to write poems as authentic as the songs he heard on Seventh Street. There, he said, was "the pulse beat of the people who keep on going."

In 1925 Hughes was working as a busboy at the Wardman Park on Connecticut Avenue, living in a room at the YMCA on 12th Street and trying to write. He had already published "The Negro Speaks of Rivers" in *Crisis* magazine in 1921. The poet Vachel Lindsay, then at the height of his fame, was staying at the Wardman Park, where he was to give a reading. Hughes shyly put three of his poems by Lindsay's place at dinner. That night at his reading, Lindsay announced that he had discovered a promising "busboy poet." Then he read the poems. Hughes, photographed in his busboy attire, became big news.

The Weary Blues appeared in 1926. Out of Hughes's Washington experience also came another collection of poems, *Fine Clothes to the Jew* (1927). The title, a reference to the many pawnshops on Seventh Street, alluded to the black life-style, one week up and wearing the fine suit, the next week down and pawning it. Some criticized Hughes for demeaning the Negro by writing in the dialect of common people. "My poems are indelicate," he agreed, "but so is life." Others, like James Baldwin, scorned him for not being angry enough.

In any case, Hughes was an original voice. Extremely prolific, he supported himself by writing; his importance to the development of black literature in America is indisputable. With a nod to Whitman, Hughes wrote, "I, too, sing America, / I am the darker brother."

STERLING BROWN (1901–1989) was Washington's beloved poet, critic, and professor of English at Howard University for forty years. He devoted his life to the development of an authentic African-American folk literature. Born across the street from Howard, where his father, Sterling Brown, Sr., was a Professor of Religion, Brown spent his youth in the neighborhood of 6th and Fairmount.

As a boy he knew all the distinguished leaders: socialist and writer W. E. B. Du Bois, critic and cultural historian Alain Locke, social historian Kelly Miller and his daughter, poet May Miller Sullivan. Through his father he met Paul Laurence Dunbar and Frederick Douglass. At prestigious Dunbar High School he got to know the bright lights of his own generation. But it was his mother who imbued him with the love of poetry. He remembers her standing over her broom, reading poetry to him.

Brown mined the rich vein of black culture, writing in the "racy idiom of humble workers," replacing caricatures with authentic folk heroes. He came to prominence during the Harlem Renaissance but wanted nothing to do with it, seeing it as a response to what the white man expected and therefore not entirely genuine.

He had an impeccable ear and could write equally well in dialect and in formal English. In 1932 the collection *Southern Road* was hailed as a breakthrough; it was seen as the work of a sophisticated poet using the real language of Negro life.

Sterling Brown was senior editor of *The Negro Caravan* (1941), the standard reference for the study of African-American literature. A

Phi Beta Kappa graduate of Williams College, in 1945 he was offered a full professorship at Vassar College, which he declined, saying of his life at Howard, "These are my people and if I had anything to give they would need it more."

In 1968, after a low period, his poetry rode the rising tide of black consciousness to a new popularity, and his books were reprinted. Honors and awards began to come his way in abundance, and in 1980 his *Collected Poems* won the Lenore Marshall Poetry Prize. In 1984, considered to be the dean of African-American poets, he was named Poet Laureate of the District of Columbia.

An elaborately courteous and immensely entertaining man, his home at 1222 Kearney Street NE in the Brookland section of Washington was an authentic salon. Writers, students, reporters, English teachers from the suburbs, a few civil rights workers, people of all races mixed together, trading ideas and enthusiasms in lively discussions under the watchful good humor of Sterling Brown.

Through the years Howard University has been a creative center and nurturer of talent, including among its graduates poet Amiri Baraka and novelist Toni Morrison (*Song of Solomon, Beloved*) who in 1993 became the first African-American to win the Nobel Prize for literature.

Founders' Library, Howard University

Greater Washington

1. F. Scott Fitzgerald: Rockville Cemetery, 600 Viers Mill Road, Rockville, Md.
2. Rachel Carson: 11701 Berwick Road, Silver Spring, Md.
3. Marjorie Kinnan Rawlings: 1221 Newton Street, NE
4. Frederick Douglass: 1411 W Street, SE
5. Ezra Pound: St. Elizabeth's Hosp., 2700 M.L.K., Jr. Blvd., SE
6. Hammett, Allen, Bemelmans: Arlington Cemetery

From earlier chapters:

7. Theodore Roosevelt Memorial: Roosevelt Island
8. James Thurber: 319 James Thurber Court, Falls Church, Va.
9. Katherine Anne Porter: 3601 49th Street, NW
10. Bruce Catton: 3139 Tennyson Street, NW
11. Joaquin Miller: present site of cabin, in Rock Creek Park
12. Adams Memorial: Rock Creek Cemetery
13. Ambrose Bierce: 14th & Euclid, NW
14. Paul Laurence Dunbar: 1934 4th Street, NW
15. Sterling Brown: 1222 Kearney Street, NE
16. Anne Royall: Congressional Cemetery, 1801 E Street, SE

Further Afield

CONSIDER THIS PLOT for a Victorian novel: Frederick Bailey is born on Maryland's Eastern Shore, the son of a white master and his slave. Separated from his family at an early age, he learns to read from the lessons given his young white master. His early experience includes grueling work as a field hand, being sold, beaten and sold again, trying to escape, being captured. In 1838, in disguise and with false papers, he takes a train north.

Always trying to stay ahead of the slave catchers, he makes his way to New Bedford, Massachusetts, where he finds work as a ship's caulker. There he changes his name to Douglass, after a character in Sir Walter Scott's *The Lady of the Lake*. And he begins to speak out.

A gifted orator, he catches the attention of William Lloyd Garrison, the abolitionist leader, and spends the next ten years traveling and speaking. He is so articulate and accomplished that some people doubt he was ever a slave.

He writes *Narrative of the Life of Frederick Douglass, an American Slave*, which brings enough fame and attention to threaten his freedom. He goes to England, where he is widely acclaimed. Friends at home raise the money to buy his freedom. He returns home, starts an abolitionist newspaper, the *North Star*, and continues to write and speak out.

In 1872 **FREDERICK DOUGLASS** (1818–1895) moved his base of operations to Washington, where he lived near the Capitol at 318 A Street NE, now the Frederick Douglass Museum and Hall of Fame for Caring Americans. This house was also the original home of the Museum of African Art, which became part of the Smithsonian in

1979. The collection is now in a grand new subterranean building on the Mall.

In 1877 Douglass moved to Cedar Hill, a handsome house at 1411 W Street SE, on a fifteen-acre estate in the Anacostia section of the city. He lived there until his death, surrounded by a large family, his books and papers, and portraits of the men in public life whom he admired. He served his country as a diplomat, held a number of government positions and was made a U. S. marshal.

Early in his career, Douglass allied himself with the cause of women's rights, perceiving that women's struggle for equality was intertwined with that of blacks. Grateful for his support, female abolitionist groups bought his freedom for $711.96. At the first National Women's Rights convention in 1850, he was elected to a national committee to help women win the right to own property and hold government positions. When the fifteenth amendment passed in 1870 with no mention of women, Douglass was anxious to show women they had not lost a champion. He worked for women's suffrage until he died.

Cedar Hill, Anacostia: Frederick Douglass

Late in life he paid a visit to a former owner, who was by then a very old man, in St. Michaels, Maryland. Douglass was himself full of years and honors, and the two men chatted amicably about the past. A life of trial and struggle, then triumph. Dickens couldn't have done it better.

Cedar Hill is open to the public on weekdays from 9 to 4 and is accessible by Tourmobile from downtown locations.

Also in the southeastern section of the city, St. Elizabeth's Hospital is situated on a hill on four hundred acres of wide lawns and flowering trees. From it **EZRA POUND** (1885–1972) could see the Capitol and the Library of Congress. It was an odd residence for a major poet, but then Pound's behavior had been odd. Living in Italy in the years before World War II, he became increasingly critical of American attitudes toward war, art, commercialism and economics. His views led him to embrace anti-Semitism, Hitler, Mussolini and fascism in general. During the war he made over three hundred radio broadcasts from Rome denouncing his country and applauding fascism.

When the American forces caught up with him after the war they arrested him and held him at Pisa in a cage (an experience which resulted in "The Pisan Cantos"). While in the cage, which was excused on the grounds that the fascists might try to rescue him, Pound read Confucius and had a very bad time. Subsequently he was brought to the United States, tried for treason and judged insane. He was placed in the criminal lunatic ward at St. Elizabeth's. It was a face-saving arrangement that permitted the United States to avoid executing one of its major creative voices.

At St. Elizabeth's Pound held bizarre court. Everyone came to call. T. S. Eliot came, and Marianne Moore and William Carlos Williams. Conrad Aiken came, and Robert Lowell, Thornton Wilder, Witter

Bynner, Tennessee Williams and Allen Tate. H. L. Mencken was appalled at the Bedlamesque conditions. When the door clanged behind him, e. e. cummings said it was the second worst experience of the kind he'd ever had, the first being his own incarceration in France during World War I. Stephen Spender, Katherine Anne Porter, Elizabeth Bishop, Langston Hughes, Louis Zukofsky, Archibald MacLeish, Randall Jarrell and James Dickey visited. Edith Hamilton brought chocolates. Robert Frost said it was where Pound belonged.

Maria St. Just described the scene: "Pound held court by the radiator. He wore khaki shorts and socks and a very white shirt. He was tremendously virile, pacing the corridors and expounding. The other patients clustered around . . . until Pound clapped his hands, shouting 'Go away' in Italian, and they all fluttered back like little birds into their cages."

When Pound was transferred from a confined ward to one with more freedom, he often played tennis on the grounds (reportedly a good net game, not much of a serve). He and his wife would sit on the lawn under the horse chestnut trees and she would read to him while the other inmates drifted around them like wraiths.

Pound was incarcerated from 1946 to 1958. The persistence of his literary friends (largely Archibald MacLeish, who used Frost as a front man because Frost was more palatable to a Republican administration) eventually won his release and he returned to Italy. From the deck of the *Cristoforo Colombo* in Naples harbor, Pound gave the fascist salute and told Italian reporters, "All America is an insane asylum."

"We are not filled with exultation that man has once more triumphed over miscreant nature," wrote **RACHEL CARSON** (1907–1964). "The 'control of nature' is a phrase conceived in arrogance."

Rachel Carson loved the woods and fields and tide pools, noticed when the whitethroats came through and later the warblers. A towering figure at the beginning of the environmental movement, she sounded the alarm. The force of her writing, her moral conviction and her mastery of facts caught the world's attention.

As a young woman in her first job at the Bureau of Fisheries, she was told to write something about the sea for a radio broadcast. Her superior handed the piece she produced back to her with a smile, saying it wasn't quite what he had in mind and please try again, and, by the way, she should submit the rejected piece to the *Atlantic Monthly*.

From that first *Atlantic Monthly* essay, Rachel Carson later recalled, everything else followed. What, she was asked, is going on in the uttermost depths of the ocean? A great many things are, according to *Under the Sea Wind* (1941). Ten years later there appeared a far more ambitious book, *The Sea around Us*. Portions of it ran in the *New Yorker* prior to publication and the reader response was greater than to any piece the magazine had ever published. By Christmas the book was selling 4,000 copies a day. It went to the top of the best seller list and remained on the list for eighty-six weeks. Ultimately it was translated into thirty-two languages.

In 1963 came *Silent Spring* which was an instant sensation. Carson's message: widespread use of untested, highly toxic chemicals was contaminating earth, air, rivers and sea on a massive scale. We were raining down death from the sky, killing mosquitoes, aphids, gypsy moths without regard for the consequences, without pausing to consider that all life is interrelated.

Just as Charles Darwin's *The Origin of Species* offended the established church more than a hundred years earlier, so *Silent Spring* offended a small but powerful piece of society—the chemical industry, the Department of Agriculture and the food and nutrition industries. They struck back, trying to discredit the book. At the same time

Carson received a mountain of mail from a horrified and supportive public.

Silent Spring is eloquent, powerful, profoundly upsetting. One cannot read this book unmoved. Moreover, Carson created a best-seller out of such a dreary subject as pesticides. A few thousand words from her and the world took a new direction.

Rachel Carson died of cancer in Silver Spring, Maryland, at the age of fifty-six in 1964. The income from her writing had enabled her to buy a modest house on an acre of land in Silver Spring at 11701 Berwick Road. Half of it she kept wild as a sanctuary for small animals and birds. Today it is still just that—a small brick house set between two brushy tangles, waiting for the whitethroats.

In April 1993 the house was designated a National Historic Landmark.

Tough-guy writer **DASHIELL HAMMETT** (1894–1961) (*The Maltese Falcon, The Glass Key, The Thin Man*) is buried in Arlington Cemetery, having served his country in both World Wars. Also buried at Arlington is **HERVEY ALLEN** (1889–1949) (*Anthony Adverse*) and **LUDWIG BEMELMANS** (1898–1962), most beloved of his books being *Madeleine*, a children's book about a little girl in Paris.

At the time of his death in December 1940, **F. SCOTT FITZGERALD's** (1896–1940) golden career was in almost total eclipse. He died in obscurity and reduced circumstances of a heart attack related to heavy drinking, in Hollywood, a town that had not been kind to him. Zelda Fitzgerald, not wanting him to be buried in California, made arrangements from her mother's home in Montgomery, Alabama, for burial just outside Washington in Rockville, Maryland, near his parents' graves.

Right after Christmas, Fitzgerald was buried in the Union Cemetery in Rockville. Because he was not a practicing Catholic at the time of his death, the church would not allow him to be buried in the family plot in St. Mary's Cemetery. About thirty people, including Scott's daughter Scottie, attended the service at a funeral home in Bethesda. Zelda was not well enough to come.

In 1948, Zelda Fitzgerald died in a sanitorium fire. A few years later the Fitzgerald revival began, and it has been going strong ever since. *This Side of Paradise* (1920), *The Great Gatsby* (1925) and *Tender Is the Night* (1934) are major American classics, and Fitzgerald himself has been the subject of a great many biographies and critical works.

In 1975, Scottie Fitzgerald Smith won permission to move Scott and Zelda to St. Mary's Churchyard (600 Viers Mill Road). There was another ceremony, with a program headed "Tender Is the Day." This

Fitzgerald's grave, Rockville Cemetery

time the media was out in force. On the gravestone is carved the last line of *The Great Gatsby:* "So we beat on, boats against the current, borne back ceaselessly into the past."

To live out of harmony with a place would be a kind of death, said **MARJORIE KINNAN RAWLINGS** (1896–1953). Although she fought against being identified as a regional writer, it was a place that caused her to catch fire as a writer.

The place wasn't Washington, where she grew up, but an old farm at Cross Creek in the central Florida scrub country. When she first saw the place, she wrote, she felt not only love but terror. She had an enormous sense of recognition, of having come home.

Before she found her muse, Marjorie Kinnan lived at 1221 Newton Street NE (the house still stands). She went to Western High School, now the Duke Ellington School for the Arts. She had been writing since childhood and at fifteen had won a prize from *McCall's* for a story. By the time she got to Florida, Rawlings was a working newspaperwoman. She immediately began to record her impressions.

A short story caught the eye of Maxwell Perkins, Scribner's fabled nourisher of talent and guider of genius. He urged her to expand the story, and the result was *South Moon Under* (1933). Perkins became Rawlings's lifelong friend and mentor; through him she met the literary elite of her time: Ernest Hemingway, Scott Fitzgerald, Thomas Wolfe, John Dos Passos.

In 1938 Rawlings published *The Yearling*, the wrenching story of a boy and a deer. It became a major bestseller and earned her literary honors, money and celebrity status. In 1942 came *Cross Creek*, another winner. Trying to move beyond regionalism, she abandoned her Florida scrub country material, her lovely place-haunted stories stopped and her writing went into a decline.

It would be unthinkable to contemplate Washington's literary life, past or present, without the journalists and columnists who have enlivened and provoked the national discourse since the early days of the Republic when Anne Royall narrowly escaped a ducking. Theirs is a noble calling, too. But where does reporting end and creativity begin? Katherine Anne Porter had an observation on that. She said, "You see, my fiction is reportage, only I do something to it. . . . And that's very hard to explain—that's the one thing you can't explain to a person who isn't a natural born fiction writer."

Further Reading

Brooks, Paul. *The House of Life: Rachel Carson at Work*. Boston: Houghton Mifflin, 1972.

Cutler, David. *Literary Washington: A Complete Guide to the Literary Life in the Nation's Capital*. Lanham: Madison Books, 1989.

Donaldson, Scott. *Archibald MacLeish: An American Life*. Boston: Houghton Mifflin, 1992.

Ellman, Richard. *Oscar Wilde*. New York: Knopf, 1984.

Fitzpatrick, Sandra and Maria R. Goodwin. *The Guide to Black Washington*. New York: Hippocrene Books, 1990.

Givner, Joan. *Katherine Anne Porter: A Life*. New York: Simon and Schuster, 1982.

Kaplan, Justin. *Walt Whitmen: A Life*. New York: Simon and Schuster, 1980.

McGuire, William. *Poetry's Catbird Seat*. Washington: Library of Congress, 1988.

Morris, Edmund. *The Rise of Theodore Roosevelt*. New York: Coward, McCann & Geoghegan, 1979.

Olson, Stanley. *Elinor Wylie: A Life Apart*. New York: Dial Press, 1979.

O'Toole, Patricia. *The Five of Hearts*. New York: Clarkson Potter, 1990.

Reid, Doris Fielding. *Edith Hamilton: An Intimate Portrait*. New York: Norton, 1967.

Schorer, Mark. *Sinclair Lewis: An American Life*. New York: McGraw Hill, 1961.

Steel, Ronald. *Walter Lippmann and the American Century*. Boston: Atlantic / Little Brown, 1980.

Thwaite, Ann. *Waiting for the Party: The Life of Frances Hodgson Burnett*. New York: Scribners, 1974.

Index